MznLnx

Missing Links Exam Preps

Exam Prep for

Principles of Customer Relationship Management

Baran, Galka, & Strunk, 1st Edition

The MznLnx Exam Prep is your link from the texbook and lecture to your exams.
The MznLnx Exam Preps are unauthorized and comprehensive reviews of your textbooks.

All material provided by MznLnx and Rico Publications (c) 2010
Textbook publishers and textbook authors do not particpate in or contribute to these reviews.

MznLnx

Rico
Publications

Exam Prep for Principles of Customer Relationship Management
1st Edition
Baran, Galka, & Strunk

Publisher: Raymond Houge
Assistant Editor: Michael Rouger
Text and Cover Designer: Lisa Buckner
Marketing Manager: Sara Swagger
Project Manager, Editorial Production: Jerry Emerson
Art Director: Vernon Lowerui

Product Manager: Dave Mason
Editorial Assitant: Rachel Guzmanji
Pedagogy: Debra Long
Cover Image: Jim Reed/Getty Images
Text and Cover Printer: City Printing, Inc.
Compositor: Media Mix, Inc.

(c) 2010 Rico Publications
ALL RIGHTS RESERVED. No part of this work covered by the copyright may be reproduced or used in any form or by an means--graphic, electronic, or mechanical, including photocopying, recording, taping, Web distribution, information storage, and retrieval systems, or in any other manner--without the written permission of the publisher.

Printed in the United States
ISBN:

For more information about our products, contact us at:
Dave.Mason@RicoPublications.com

For permission to use material from this text or product, submit a request online to:
Dave.Mason@RicoPublications.com

Contents

CHAPTER 1
Introduction to Customer Relationship Management   1

CHAPTER 2
History and Development of CRM   8

CHAPTER 3
Relationship Marketing and Customer Relationship Management   14

CHAPTER 4
Organization and CRM   18

CHAPTER 5
CRM and Data Management   21

CHAPTER 6
Technology and Data Platforms   24

CHAPTER 7
Database and Customer Data Development   28

CHAPTER 8
Sales Strategy and CRM   31

CHAPTER 9
CRM Technology and Sales   35

CHAPTER 10
Marketing Strategy and CRM   38

CHAPTER 11
CRM, Marketing Automation, and Communication   44

CHAPTER 12
CRM Program Measurement and Tools   46

CHAPTER 13
Privacy and Ethics Considerations   53

CHAPTER 14
The Future of CRM   57

ANSWER KEY   59

TO THE STUDENT

COMPREHENSIVE

The *MznLnx* Exam Prep series is designed to help you pass your exams. Editors at MznLnx review your textbooks and then prepare these practice exams to help you master the textbook material. Unlike study guides, workbooks, and practice tests provided by the texbook publisher and textbook authors, *MznLnx* gives you **all** of the material in each chapter in exam form, not just samples, so you can be sure to nail your exam.

MECHANICAL

The MznLnx Exam Prep series creates exams that will help you learn the subject matter as well as test you on your understanding. Each question is designed to help you master the concept. Just working through the exams, you gain an understanding of the subject--its a simple mechanical process that produces success.

INTEGRATED STUDY GUIDE AND REVIEW

MznLnx is not just a set of exams designed to test you, its also a comprehensive review of the subject content. Each exam question is also a review of the concept, making sure that you will get the answer correct without having to go to other sources of material. You learn as you go! Its the easiest way to pass an exam.

HUMOR

Studying can be tedious and dry. MznLnx's instructional design includes moderate humor within the exam questions on occassion, to break the tedium and revitalize the brain

Chapter 1. Introduction to Customer Relationship Management

1. _____ is the process by which a new idea or new product is accepted by the market. The rate of _____ is the speed that the new idea spreads from one consumer to the next. Adoption is similar to _____ except that it deals with the psychological processes an individual goes through, rather than an aggregate market process.

   a. Diffusion
   b. Market development
   c. Kano model
   d. Perceptual maps

2. _____ describes activities of businesses serving end consumers with products and/or services.

   An example of a B2C transaction would be a person buying a pair of shoes from a retailer. The transactions that led to the shoes being available for purchase, that is the purchase of the leather, laces, rubber, etc.

   a. Societal marketing
   b. Business-to-consumer
   c. Corporate capabilities package
   d. Demand generation

3. _____ is a method used for analyzing customer behavior and defining market segments. It is commonly used in database marketing and direct marketing and has received particular attention in retail.

   _____ stands for

   - Recency - When was the last order?
   - Frequency - How many orders have they placed with us?
   - Monetary Value - What is the value of their orders?

   To create an _____ analysis, one creates categories for each attribute. For instance, the Recency attribute might be broken into three categories: customers with purchases within the last 90 days; between 91 and 365 days; and longer than 365 days.

   a. Trade credit
   b. Merchant
   c. Retail loss prevention
   d. RFM

4. _____ is defined by the Oxford English Dictionary as 'the action or practice of selling among or between established clients, markets, traders, etc.' or 'that of selling an additional product or service to an existing customer'. In practice businesses define _____ in many different ways. Elements that might influence the definition might include: the size of the business, the industry sector it operates within and the financial motivations of those required to define the term.

Chapter 1. Introduction to Customer Relationship Management

a. Yield management
b. Freebie marketing
c. Service provider
d. Cross-selling

5. _____ is defined by the American _____ Association as the activity, set of institutions, and processes for creating, communicating, delivering, and exchanging offerings that have value for customers, clients, partners, and society at large. The term developed from the original meaning which referred literally to going to market, as in shopping, or going to a market to sell goods or services.

_____ practice tends to be seen as a creative industry, which includes advertising, distribution and selling.

a. Marketing
b. Marketing myopia
c. Product naming
d. Customer acquisition management

6. _____ is a form of marketing developed from direct response marketing campaigns conducted in the 1970's and 1980's which emphasizes customer retention and satisfaction, rather than a dominant focus on 'point of sale' transactions.

_____ differs from other forms of marketing in that it recognizes the long term value to the firm of keeping customers, as opposed to direct or 'Intrusion' marketing, which focuses upon acquisition of new clients by targeting majority demographics based upon prospective client lists.

_____ refers to long-term and mutually beneficial arrangement wherein both buyer and seller focus on value enhancement through the certain of more satisfying exchange. This approach attempts to transcend the simple purchase exchange process with customer to make more meaningful and richer contact by providing a more holistic, personalized purchase, and use orn consumption experience to create stronger ties.

a. Relationship marketing
b. Guerrilla Marketing
c. Global marketing
d. Diversity marketing

7. _____ is the sum of all experiences a customer has with a supplier of goods or services, over the duration of their relationship with that supplier. It can also be used to mean an individual experience over one transaction; the distinction is usually clear in context.

Analysts and commentators who write about _____ and CRM have increasingly recognized the importance of managing the customer's experience.

a. Customer service
b. Customer Integrated System
c. COPC Inc.
d. Customer experience

8. A _____ is a plan of action designed to achieve a particular goal.

_____ is different from tactics. In military terms, tactics is concerned with the conduct of an engagement while _____ is concerned with how different engagements are linked.

a. 6-3-5 Brainwriting
b. 180SearchAssistant
c. Power III
d. Strategy

9. In the field of computer security, _____ is the criminally fraudulent process of attempting to acquire sensitive information such as usernames, passwords and credit card details by masquerading as a trustworthy entity in an electronic communication. Communications purporting to be from popular social web sites, auction sites, online payment processors or IT Administrators are commonly used to lure the unsuspecting public. _____ is typically carried out by e-mail or instant messaging, and it often directs users to enter details at a fake website whose look and feel are almost identical to the legitimate one.

a. Directory Harvest Attack
b. Phishing
c. Telemarketing
d. Joe job

10. _____ refer to a collection of facts usually collected as the result of experience, observation or experiment or a set of premises. This may consist of numbers, words particularly as measurements or observations of a set of variables. _____ are often viewed as a lowest level of abstraction from which information and knowledge are derived.

a. Sample size
b. Data
c. Pearson product-moment correlation coefficient
d. Mean

Chapter 1. Introduction to Customer Relationship Management

11. A _____ is a process that can allow an organization to concentrate its limited resources on the greatest opportunities to increase sales and achieve a sustainable competitive advantage. A _____ should be centered around the key concept that customer satisfaction is the main goal.

A _____ is most effective when it is an integral component of corporate strategy, defining how the organization will successfully engage customers, prospects, and competitors in the market arena.

   a. Psychographic
   b. Cyberdoc
   c. Marketing strategy
   d. Societal marketing

12. Radio-frequency identification (_____) is the use of an object (typically referred to as an _____ tag) applied to or incorporated into a product, animal, or person for the purpose of identification and tracking using radio waves. Some tags can be read from several meters away and beyond the line of sight of the reader.

Most _____ tags contain at least two parts.

   a. Power III
   b. 6-3-5 Brainwriting
   c. 180SearchAssistant
   d. RFID

13. _____ refers to marketing strategies applied directly to a specific consumer.

Having the knowledge on the consumer preferences, there are suggested personalized products and promotions to each consumer.

The _____ is based in four main steps in order to fulfill its goals: Those stages are identify, differentiate, interact, and customize.

   a. One-to-one marketing
   b. ACNielsen
   c. AMAX
   d. ADTECH

14. On an intranet or B2E Enterprise Web portals, personalization is often based on user attributes such as department, functional area, or role. The term _____ in this context refers to the ability of users to modify the page layout or specify what content should be displayed.

There are two categories of personalizations:

1. Rule-based
2. Content-based

Web personalization models include rules-based filtering, based on 'if this, then that' rules processing, and collaborative filtering, which serves relevant material to customers by combining their own personal preferences with the preferences of like-minded others. Collaborative filtering works well for books, music, video, etc.

a. Self branding
b. Cashmere Agency
c. Movin'
d. Customization

15. _____ is the process of extracting hidden patterns from data. As more data is gathered, with the amount of data doubling every three years, _____ is becoming an increasingly important tool to transform this data into information. It is commonly used in a wide range of profiling practices, such as marketing, surveillance, fraud detection and scientific discovery.
   a. Power III
   b. 180SearchAssistant
   c. Structure mining
   d. Data mining

16. _____ is marketing using many different marketing channels to reach a customer. In this sense, a channel might be a retail store, a web site, a mail order catalogue, or direct personal communications by letter, email or text message. The objective of the company doing the marketing is to make it easy for a consumer to buy from them in whatever way is most appropriate.
   a. Buy one, get one free
   b. Blitz QFD
   c. Macromarketing
   d. Multichannel marketing

17. Sales force management systems are information systems used in marketing and management that help automate some sales and sales force management functions. They are frequently combined with a marketing information system, in which case they are often called Customer Relationship Management (CRM) systems.

_____ Systems, typically a part of a company's customer relationship management system, is a system that automatically records all the stages in a sales process.

a. 6-3-5 Brainwriting
b. Power III
c. 180SearchAssistant
d. Sales force automation

18. The term _____ refers to several methods by which individuals can avoid receiving unsolicited product or service information. This ability is usually associated with direct marketing campaigns such as telemarketing, e-mail marketing, or direct mail.

The U.S. Federal Government created the National Do Not Call Registry to reduce the telemarketing calls consumers receive at home.

a. ADTECH
b. AMAX
c. ACNielsen
d. Opt-out

19. _____ or personalisation is tailoring a consumer product, electronic or written medium to a user based on personal details or characteristics they provide. More recently, it has especially been applied in the context of the World Wide Web.

Web pages are personalized based on the interests of an individual.

a. Sexism,
b. Flighting
c. Complex sale
d. Personalization

20. _____ is the ability of an individual or group to seclude themselves or information about themselves and thereby reveal themselves selectively. The boundaries and content of what is considered private differ among cultures and individuals, but share basic common themes. _____ is sometimes related to anonymity, the wish to remain unnoticed or unidentified in the public realm.
a. 180SearchAssistant
b. 6-3-5 Brainwriting
c. Privacy
d. Power III

Chapter 1. Introduction to Customer Relationship Management

21. _____ is a market coverage strategy in which a firm decides to ignore market segment differences and go after the whole market with one offer.it is type of marketing (or attempting to sell through persuasion) of a product to a wide audience. The idea is to broadcast a message that will reach the largest number of people possible. Traditionally _____ has focused on radio, television and newspapers as the medium used to reach this broad audience.
    a. Marketspace
    b. Business-to-consumer
    c. Cyberdoc
    d. Mass marketing

22. _____, in marketing, manufacturing, and management, is the use of flexible computer-aided manufacturing systems to produce custom output. Those systems combine the low unit costs of mass production processes with the flexibility of individual customization.

    '_____' is the new frontier in business competition for both manufacturing and service industries.

    a. Vertical integration
    b. Mass customization
    c. Power III
    d. Flanking marketing warfare strategies

23. _____ is a measure of the strength of a brand, product, service relative to competitive offerings. There is often a geographic element to the competitive landscape. In defining _____, you must see to what extent a product, brand, or firm controls a product category in a given geographic area.
    a. Discretionary spending
    b. Market system
    c. Market dominance
    d. Productivity

Chapter 2. History and Development of CRM

1. _____ is defined by the American _____ Association as the activity, set of institutions, and processes for creating, communicating, delivering, and exchanging offerings that have value for customers, clients, partners, and society at large. The term developed from the original meaning which referred literally to going to market, as in shopping, or going to a market to sell goods or services.

_____ practice tends to be seen as a creative industry, which includes advertising, distribution and selling.

   a. Product naming
   b. Customer acquisition management
   c. Marketing
   d. Marketing myopia

2. _____ is a form of marketing developed from direct response marketing campaigns conducted in the 1970's and 1980's which emphasizes customer retention and satisfaction, rather than a dominant focus on 'point of sale' transactions.

_____ differs from other forms of marketing in that it recognizes the long term value to the firm of keeping customers, as opposed to direct or 'Intrusion' marketing, which focuses upon acquisition of new clients by targeting majority demographics based upon prospective client lists.

_____ refers to long-term and mutually beneficial arrangement wherein both buyer and seller focus on value enhancement through the certain of more satisfying exchange. This approach attempts to transcend the simple purchase exchange process with customer to make more meaningful and richer contact by providing a more holistic, personalized purchase, and use orn consumption experience to create stronger ties.

   a. Global marketing
   b. Guerrilla Marketing
   c. Diversity marketing
   d. Relationship marketing

3. A _____ is a plan of action designed to achieve a particular goal.

_____ is different from tactics. In military terms, tactics is concerned with the conduct of an engagement while _____ is concerned with how different engagements are linked.

   a. Strategy
   b. 6-3-5 Brainwriting
   c. Power III
   d. 180SearchAssistant

Chapter 2. History and Development of CRM

4. Consumer market research is a form of applied sociology that concentrates on understanding the behaviours, whims and preferences, of consumers in a market-based economy, and aims to understand the effects and comparative success of marketing campaigns. The field of consumer _____ as a statistical science was pioneered by Arthur Nielsen with the founding of the ACNielsen Company in 1923.

Thus _____ is the systematic and objective identification, collection, analysis, and dissemination of information for the purpose of assisting management in decision making related to the identification and solution of problems and opportunities in marketing.

   a. Logit analysis
   b. Focus group
   c. Marketing research process
   d. Marketing research

5. Radio-frequency identification (_____) is the use of an object (typically referred to as an _____ tag) applied to or incorporated into a product, animal, or person for the purpose of identification and tracking using radio waves. Some tags can be read from several meters away and beyond the line of sight of the reader.

Most _____ tags contain at least two parts.

   a. 6-3-5 Brainwriting
   b. 180SearchAssistant
   c. RFID
   d. Power III

6. _____ in organizations and public policy is both the organizational process of creating and maintaining a plan; and the psychological process of thinking about the activities required to create a desired goal on some scale. As such, it is a fundamental property of intelligent behavior. This thought process is essential to the creation and refinement of a plan, or integration of it with other plans, that is, it combines forecasting of developments with the preparation of scenarios of how to react to them.
   a. Power III
   b. 180SearchAssistant
   c. Planning
   d. 6-3-5 Brainwriting

7. A _____ is a structured collection of records or data that is stored in a computer system. The structure is achieved by organizing the data according to a _____ model. The model in most common use today is the relational model.

a. 180SearchAssistant
b. 6-3-5 Brainwriting
c. Power III
d. Database

8. _____ is the process by which a new idea or new product is accepted by the market. The rate of _____ is the speed that the new idea spreads from one consumer to the next. Adoption is similar to _____ except that it deals with the psychological processes an individual goes through, rather than an aggregate market process.

a. Market development
b. Perceptual maps
c. Diffusion
d. Kano model

9. _____ is a form of direct marketing using databases of customers or potential customers to generate personalized communications in order to promote a product or service for marketing purposes. The method of communication can be any addressable medium, as in direct marketing.

The distinction between direct and _____ stems primarily from the attention paid to the analysis of data.

a. Power III
b. Direct marketing
c. Database marketing
d. Direct Marketing Associations

10. _____ is an advertisement in which a particular product specifically mentions a competitor by name for the express purpose of showing why the competitor is inferior to the product naming it.

This should not be confused with parody advertisements, where a fictional product is being advertised for the purpose of poking fun at the particular advertisement, nor should it be confused with the use of a coined brand name for the purpose of comparing the product without actually naming an actual competitor. ('Wikipedia tastes better and is less filling than the Encyclopedia Galactica.')

In the 1980s, during what has been referred to as the cola wars, soft-drink manufacturer Pepsi ran a series of advertisements where people, caught on hidden camera, in a blind taste test, chose Pepsi over rival Coca-Cola.

Chapter 2. History and Development of CRM

a. Heavy-up
b. Cost per conversion
c. Comparative advertising
d. GL-70

11. _____ is marketing based on relationship and value. It may be used to market a service or a product.

Marketing a service-base business is different from marketing a goods-base business.

a. 6-3-5 Brainwriting
b. Services marketing
c. Power III
d. 180SearchAssistant

12. _____ is a method used for analyzing customer behavior and defining market segments. It is commonly used in database marketing and direct marketing and has received particular attention in retail.

_____ stands for

- Recency - When was the last order?
- Frequency - How many orders have they placed with us?
- Monetary Value - What is the value of their orders?

To create an _____ analysis, one creates categories for each attribute. For instance, the Recency attribute might be broken into three categories: customers with purchases within the last 90 days; between 91 and 365 days; and longer than 365 days.

a. Retail loss prevention
b. RFM
c. Trade credit
d. Merchant

13. _____ is defined by the Oxford English Dictionary as 'the action or practice of selling among or between established clients, markets, traders, etc.' or 'that of selling an additional product or service to an existing customer'. In practice businesses define _____ in many different ways. Elements that might influence the definition might include: the size of the business, the industry sector it operates within and the financial motivations of those required to define the term.

a. Freebie marketing
b. Service provider
c. Yield management
d. Cross-selling

14. _____ refers to messages and related media used to communicate with a market. Those who practice advertising, branding, direct marketing, graphic design, marketing, packaging, promotion, publicity, sponsorship, public relations, sales, sales promotion and online marketing are termed marketing communicators, _____ managers, or more briefly as marcom managers.
   a. Merchandise
   b. Sales promotion
   c. Merchandising
   d. Marketing communication

15. A _____ attribute is one that exists in a range of magnitudes, and can therefore be measured. Measurements of any particular _____ property are expressed as a specific quantity, referred to as a unit, multiplied by a number. Examples of physical quantities are distance, mass, and time.
   a. BeyondROI
   b. Quantitative
   c. Lifestyle city
   d. Dolly Dimples

16. _____ is a process by which data from customer behavior is used to help make key business decisions via market segmentation and predictive analytics. This information is used by businesses for direct marketing, site selection, and customer relationship management.

RetailGathering customer data and implementing it into some type of application that can enhance insight and the decision making process is a common application of _____ used by retailers.

   a. Customer analytics
   b. Cyberdoc
   c. Disruptive technology
   d. Societal marketing

17. A _____ is a process that can allow an organization to concentrate its limited resources on the greatest opportunities to increase sales and achieve a sustainable competitive advantage. A _____ should be centered around the key concept that customer satisfaction is the main goal.

A _____ is most effective when it is an integral component of corporate strategy, defining how the organization will successfully engage customers, prospects, and competitors in the market arena.

a. Societal marketing
b. Psychographic
c. Cyberdoc
d. Marketing strategy

18. In the field of computer security, _____ is the criminally fraudulent process of attempting to acquire sensitive information such as usernames, passwords and credit card details by masquerading as a trustworthy entity in an electronic communication. Communications purporting to be from popular social web sites, auction sites, online payment processors or IT Administrators are commonly used to lure the unsuspecting public. _____ is typically carried out by e-mail or instant messaging, and it often directs users to enter details at a fake website whose look and feel are almost identical to the legitimate one.

a. Joe job
b. Directory Harvest Attack
c. Telemarketing
d. Phishing

Chapter 3. Relationship Marketing and Customer Relationship Management

1. _____ is defined by the American _____ Association as the activity, set of institutions, and processes for creating, communicating, delivering, and exchanging offerings that have value for customers, clients, partners, and society at large. The term developed from the original meaning which referred literally to going to market, as in shopping, or going to a market to sell goods or services.

_____ practice tends to be seen as a creative industry, which includes advertising, distribution and selling.

   a. Marketing myopia
   b. Product naming
   c. Customer acquisition management
   d. Marketing

2. _____ is a form of marketing developed from direct response marketing campaigns conducted in the 1970's and 1980's which emphasizes customer retention and satisfaction, rather than a dominant focus on 'point of sale' transactions.

_____ differs from other forms of marketing in that it recognizes the long term value to the firm of keeping customers, as opposed to direct or 'Intrusion' marketing, which focuses upon acquisition of new clients by targeting majority demographics based upon prospective client lists.

_____ refers to long-term and mutually beneficial arrangement wherein both buyer and seller focus on value enhancement through the certain of more satisfying exchange. This approach attempts to transcend the simple purchase exchange process with customer to make more meaningful and richer contact by providing a more holistic, personalized purchase, and use orn consumption experience to create stronger ties.

   a. Relationship marketing
   b. Diversity marketing
   c. Global marketing
   d. Guerrilla Marketing

3. A _____ is a plan of action designed to achieve a particular goal.

_____ is different from tactics. In military terms, tactics is concerned with the conduct of an engagement while _____ is concerned with how different engagements are linked.

   a. Strategy
   b. 6-3-5 Brainwriting
   c. Power III
   d. 180SearchAssistant

Chapter 3. Relationship Marketing and Customer Relationship Management

4. In the field of computer security, _____ is the criminally fraudulent process of attempting to acquire sensitive information such as usernames, passwords and credit card details by masquerading as a trustworthy entity in an electronic communication. Communications purporting to be from popular social web sites, auction sites, online payment processors or IT Administrators are commonly used to lure the unsuspecting public. _____ is typically carried out by e-mail or instant messaging, and it often directs users to enter details at a fake website whose look and feel are almost identical to the legitimate one.
   a. Directory Harvest Attack
   b. Phishing
   c. Telemarketing
   d. Joe job

5. The _____ is generally accepted as the use and specification of the four p's describing the strategic position of a product in the marketplace. One version of the origins of the _____ starts in 1948 when James Culliton said that a marketing decision should be a result of something similar to a recipe. This version continued in 1953 when Neil Borden, in his American Marketing Association presidential address, took the recipe idea one step further and coined the term 'Marketing-Mix'.
   a. Power III
   b. Marketing mix
   c. 6-3-5 Brainwriting
   d. 180SearchAssistant

6. _____ is a method used for analyzing customer behavior and defining market segments. It is commonly used in database marketing and direct marketing and has received particular attention in retail.

_____ stands for

- Recency - When was the last order?
- Frequency - How many orders have they placed with us?
- Monetary Value - What is the value of their orders?

To create an _____ analysis, one creates categories for each attribute. For instance, the Recency attribute might be broken into three categories: customers with purchases within the last 90 days; between 91 and 365 days; and longer than 365 days.

   a. Retail loss prevention
   b. Trade credit
   c. Merchant
   d. RFM

Chapter 3. Relationship Marketing and Customer Relationship Management

7. _____ is defined by the Oxford English Dictionary as 'the action or practice of selling among or between established clients, markets, traders, etc.' or 'that of selling an additional product or service to an existing customer'. In practice businesses define _____ in many different ways. Elements that might influence the definition might include: the size of the business, the industry sector it operates within and the financial motivations of those required to define the term.
   a. Freebie marketing
   b. Yield management
   c. Service provider
   d. Cross-selling

8. Radio-frequency identification (_____) is the use of an object (typically referred to as an _____ tag) applied to or incorporated into a product, animal, or person for the purpose of identification and tracking using radio waves. Some tags can be read from several meters away and beyond the line of sight of the reader.

Most _____ tags contain at least two parts.

   a. RFID
   b. 180SearchAssistant
   c. Power III
   d. 6-3-5 Brainwriting

9. _____ is a sub-discipline and type of marketing. There are two main definitional characteristics which distinguish it from other types of marketing. The first is that it attempts to send its messages directly to consumers, without the use of intervening media.
   a. Power III
   b. Direct Marketing Associations
   c. Database marketing
   d. Direct marketing

10. _____ refers to several different marketing arrangements:

_____ is when two companies form an alliance to work together, creating marketing synergy. As described in _____: The Science of Alliance:

_____ is an arrangement that associates a single product or service with more than one brand name, or otherwise associates a product with someone other than the principal producer. The typical _____ agreement involves two or more companies acting in cooperation to associate any of various logos, color schemes, or brand identifiers to a specific product that is contractually designated for this purpose.

Chapter 3. Relationship Marketing and Customer Relationship Management

a. Brand Development Index
b. Target audience
c. Co-branding
d. Line extension

11. A _____ is a process that can allow an organization to concentrate its limited resources on the greatest opportunities to increase sales and achieve a sustainable competitive advantage. A _____ should be centered around the key concept that customer satisfaction is the main goal.

A _____ is most effective when it is an integral component of corporate strategy, defining how the organization will successfully engage customers, prospects, and competitors in the market arena.

a. Cyberdoc
b. Psychographic
c. Marketing strategy
d. Societal marketing

Chapter 4. Organization and CRM

1. _____ is difficult to define. For example, in 1952, Alfred Kroeber and Clyde Kluckhohn compiled a list of 164 definitions of '_____' in _____: A Critical Review of Concepts and Definitions. However, the word '_____' is most commonly used in three basic senses:

- excellence of taste in the fine arts and humanities
- an integrated pattern of human knowledge, belief, and behavior that depends upon the capacity for symbolic thought and social learning
- the set of shared attitudes, values, goals, and practices that characterizes an institution, organization or group.

When the concept first emerged in eighteenth- and nineteenth-century Europe, it connoted a process of cultivation or improvement, as in agriculture or horticulture. In the nineteenth century, it came to refer first to the betterment or refinement of the individual, especially through education, and then to the fulfillment of national aspirations or ideals.

   a. AStore
   b. Albert Einstein
   c. African Americans
   d. Culture

2. A _____ is a collection of symbols, experiences and associations connected with a product, a service, a person or any other artifact or entity.

_____s have become increasingly important components of culture and the economy, now being described as 'cultural accessories and personal philosophies'.

Some people distinguish the psychological aspect of a _____ from the experiential aspect.

   a. Brandable software
   b. Brand equity
   c. Brand
   d. Store brand

3. _____ is the study of the Earth and its lands, features, inhabitants, and phenomena. A literal translation would be 'to describe or write about the Earth'. The first person to use the word '_____' was Eratosthenes .
   a. 6-3-5 Brainwriting
   b. Power III
   c. 180SearchAssistant
   d. Geography

4. An _____ is the manufacturing of a good or service within a category. Although _____ is a broad term for any kind of economic production, in economics and urban planning _____ is a synonym for the secondary sector, which is a type of economic activity involved in the manufacturing of raw materials into goods and products.

There are four key industrial economic sectors: the primary sector, largely raw material extraction industries such as mining and farming; the secondary sector, involving refining, construction, and manufacturing; the tertiary sector, which deals with services (such as law and medicine) and distribution of manufactured goods; and the quaternary sector, a relatively new type of knowledge _____ focusing on technological research, design and development such as computer programming, and biochemistry.

  a. ACNielsen
  b. AMAX
  c. ADTECH
  d. Industry

5. A personal and cultural _____ is a relative ethic _____, an assumption upon which implementation can be extrapolated. A _____ system is a set of consistent _____s and measures that is soo not true. A principle _____ is a foundation upon which other _____s and measures of integrity are based.
  a. Perceptual maps
  b. Package-on-Package
  c. Supreme Court of the United States
  d. Value

6. The _____ is a concept from business management that was first described and popularized by Michael Porter in his 1985 best-seller, Competitive Advantage: Creating and Sustaining Superior Performance.

A _____ is a chain of activities. Products pass through all activities of the chain in order and at each activity the product gains some value.

  a. Mass marketing
  b. Business-to-business
  c. Relationship management
  d. Value chain

7. _____ comprises a range of practices used in an organisation to identify, create, represent, distribute and enable adoption of insights and experiences. Such insights and experiences comprise knowledge, either embodied in individuals or embedded in organisational processes or practice. An established discipline since 1991 , _____ includes courses taught in the fields of business administration, information systems, management, and library and information sciences .

a. 180SearchAssistant
b. Power III
c. 6-3-5 Brainwriting
d. Knowledge management

1. _____ refer to a collection of facts usually collected as the result of experience, observation or experiment or a set of premises. This may consist of numbers, words particularly as measurements or observations of a set of variables. _____ are often viewed as a lowest level of abstraction from which information and knowledge are derived.

   a. Mean
   b. Pearson product-moment correlation coefficient
   c. Sample size
   d. Data

2. _____ is the provision of service to customers before, during and after a purchase.

   According to Turban et al., '_____ is a series of activities designed to enhance the level of customer satisfaction - that is, the feeling that a product or service has met the customer expectation.'

   Its importance varies by product, industry and customer.

   a. Customer experience
   b. COPC Inc.
   c. Facing
   d. Customer service

3. In statistics, an _____ is a term in a statistical model added when the effect of two or more variables is not simply additive. Such a term reflects that the effect of one variable depends on the values of one or more other variables.

   Thus, for a response Y and two variables x_1 and x_2 an additive model would be:

   $$Y = ax_1 + bx_2 + \text{error}$$

   In contrast to this,

   $$Y = ax_1 + bx_2 + c(x_1 \times x_2) + \text{error},$$

   is an example of a model with an _____ between variables x_1 and x_2 ('error' refers to the random variable whose value by which y differs from the expected value of y.)

   a. Interaction
   b. ADTECH
   c. AMAX
   d. ACNielsen

Chapter 5. CRM and Data Management

4. _____ is an advertisement in which a particular product specifically mentions a competitor by name for the express purpose of showing why the competitor is inferior to the product naming it.

This should not be confused with parody advertisements, where a fictional product is being advertised for the purpose of poking fun at the particular advertisement, nor should it be confused with the use of a coined brand name for the purpose of comparing the product without actually naming an actual competitor. ('Wikipedia tastes better and is less filling than the Encyclopedia Galactica.')

In the 1980s, during what has been referred to as the cola wars, soft-drink manufacturer Pepsi ran a series of advertisements where people, caught on hidden camera, in a blind taste test, chose Pepsi over rival Coca-Cola.

   a. Heavy-up
   b. Cost per conversion
   c. Comparative advertising
   d. GL-70

5. _____ is one of the four elements of marketing mix. An organization or set of organizations (go-betweens) involved in the process of making a product or service available for use or consumption by a consumer or business user.

The other three parts of the marketing mix are product, pricing, and promotion.

   a. Japan Advertising Photographers' Association
   b. Better Living Through Chemistry
   c. Comparison-Shopping agent
   d. Distribution

6. A _____ is a structured collection of records or data that is stored in a computer system. The structure is achieved by organizing the data according to a _____ model. The model in most common use today is the relational model.
   a. Power III
   b. 180SearchAssistant
   c. 6-3-5 Brainwriting
   d. Database

7. _____ describes activities of businesses serving end consumers with products and/or services.

An example of a B2C transaction would be a person buying a pair of shoes from a retailer. The transactions that led to the shoes being available for purchase, that is the purchase of the leather, laces, rubber, etc.

a. Corporate capabilities package
b. Demand generation
c. Societal marketing
d. Business-to-consumer

8. _____ is a term used to describe a process of preparing and collecting data - for example as part of a process improvement or similar project.

_____ usually takes place early on in an improvement project, and is often formalised through a _____ Plan which often contains the following activity.

1. Pre collection activity - Agree goals, target data, definitions, methods
2. Collection - _____
3. Present Findings - usually involves some form of sorting analysis and/or presentation.

A formal _____ process is necessary as it ensures that data gathered is both defined and accurate and that subsequent decisions based on arguments embodied in the findings are valid . The process provides both a baseline from which to measure from and in certain cases a target on what to improve. Types of _____ 1-By mail questionnaires 2-By personal interview

- Six sigma
- Sampling (statistics)

a. 180SearchAssistant
b. Power III
c. 6-3-5 Brainwriting
d. Data collection

9. In the field of computer security, _____ is the criminally fraudulent process of attempting to acquire sensitive information such as usernames, passwords and credit card details by masquerading as a trustworthy entity in an electronic communication. Communications purporting to be from popular social web sites, auction sites, online payment processors or IT Administrators are commonly used to lure the unsuspecting public. _____ is typically carried out by e-mail or instant messaging, and it often directs users to enter details at a fake website whose look and feel are almost identical to the legitimate one.
a. Telemarketing
b. Directory Harvest Attack
c. Joe job
d. Phishing

Chapter 6. Technology and Data Platforms

1. _____ refer to a collection of facts usually collected as the result of experience, observation or experiment or a set of premises. This may consist of numbers, words particularly as measurements or observations of a set of variables. _____ are often viewed as a lowest level of abstraction from which information and knowledge are derived.
   a. Sample size
   b. Pearson product-moment correlation coefficient
   c. Mean
   d. Data

2. Radio-frequency identification (_____) is the use of an object (typically referred to as an _____ tag) applied to or incorporated into a product, animal, or person for the purpose of identification and tracking using radio waves. Some tags can be read from several meters away and beyond the line of sight of the reader.

   Most _____ tags contain at least two parts.

   a. 6-3-5 Brainwriting
   b. Power III
   c. 180SearchAssistant
   d. RFID

3. A _____ is a structured collection of records or data that is stored in a computer system. The structure is achieved by organizing the data according to a _____ model. The model in most common use today is the relational model.
   a. 180SearchAssistant
   b. 6-3-5 Brainwriting
   c. Power III
   d. Database

4. _____ is a form of direct marketing using databases of customers or potential customers to generate personalized communications in order to promote a product or service for marketing purposes. The method of communication can be any addressable medium, as in direct marketing.

   The distinction between direct and _____ stems primarily from the attention paid to the analysis of data.

   a. Power III
   b. Direct marketing
   c. Direct Marketing Associations
   d. Database marketing

Chapter 6. Technology and Data Platforms

5. _____ is defined by the American _____ Association as the activity, set of institutions, and processes for creating, communicating, delivering, and exchanging offerings that have value for customers, clients, partners, and society at large. The term developed from the original meaning which referred literally to going to market, as in shopping, or going to a market to sell goods or services.

_____ practice tends to be seen as a creative industry, which includes advertising, distribution and selling.

a. Product naming
b. Marketing myopia
c. Customer acquisition management
d. Marketing

6. _____ is a market coverage strategy in which a firm decides to ignore market segment differences and go after the whole market with one offer.it is type of marketing (or attempting to sell through persuasion) of a product to a wide audience. The idea is to broadcast a message that will reach the largest number of people possible. Traditionally _____ has focused on radio, television and newspapers as the medium used to reach this broad audience.
a. Marketspace
b. Mass marketing
c. Cyberdoc
d. Business-to-consumer

7. _____ is the term used to describe the academic study of the various means by which individuals and entities relay information through mass media to large segments of the population at the same time. It is usually understood to relate to newspaper and magazine publishing, radio, television and film, as these are used both for disseminating news and for advertising.

_____ research includes media institutions and processes such as diffusion of information, and media effects such as persuasion or manipulation of public opinion.

a. 180SearchAssistant
b. Power III
c. Mass communication
d. 6-3-5 Brainwriting

8. A _____ is a plan of action designed to achieve a particular goal.

_____ is different from tactics. In military terms, tactics is concerned with the conduct of an engagement while _____ is concerned with how different engagements are linked.

Chapter 6. Technology and Data Platforms

a. Power III
b. 6-3-5 Brainwriting
c. 180SearchAssistant
d. Strategy

9. In the field of computer security, _____ is the criminally fraudulent process of attempting to acquire sensitive information such as usernames, passwords and credit card details by masquerading as a trustworthy entity in an electronic communication. Communications purporting to be from popular social web sites, auction sites, online payment processors or IT Administrators are commonly used to lure the unsuspecting public. _____ is typically carried out by e-mail or instant messaging, and it often directs users to enter details at a fake website whose look and feel are almost identical to the legitimate one.
   a. Joe job
   b. Telemarketing
   c. Directory Harvest Attack
   d. Phishing

10. _____ is a recursive process where two or more people or organizations work together toward an intersection of common goals -- for example, an intellectual endeavor that is creative in nature--by sharing knowledge, learning and building consensus. _____ does not require leadership and can sometimes bring better results through decentralization and egalitarianism. In particular, teams that work collaboratively can obtain greater resources, recognition and reward when facing competition for finite resources._____ is also present in opposing goals exhibiting the notion of adversarial _____, though this notion is atypical of the annotation that people have given towards their understanding of _____.
   a. 6-3-5 Brainwriting
   b. 180SearchAssistant
   c. Power III
   d. Collaboration

11. _____ , according to The American Marketing Association, is 'a planning process designed to assure that all brand contacts received by a customer or prospect for a product, service, or organization are relevant to that person and consistent over time.' (Marketing Power Dictionary)

_____ is a term used to describe a holistic approach to marketing. It aims to ensure consistency of message and the complementary use of media. The concept includes online and offline marketing channels.

a. AMAX
b. ADTECH
c. ACNielsen
d. Integrated marketing communications

12. In economics, an externality or spillover of an economic transaction is an impact on a party that is not directly involved in the transaction. In such a case, prices do not reflect the full costs or benefits in production or consumption of a product or service. A positive impact is called an _____ benefit, while a negative impact is called an _____ cost.
    a. ACNielsen
    b. ADTECH
    c. AMAX
    d. External

13. _____ is a technical term used in management science popularized by Joseph M. Juran

He defined an internal and external customers as anyone affected by the product or by the process used to produce the product, in the context of quality management. _____s may play the role as supplier, processer, and customer in the sequence of product development.

He claimed that the organization must understand and identify both internal and external customers and their needs.

    a. AMAX
    b. Internal customer
    c. ACNielsen
    d. ADTECH

14. In economics, business, retail, and accounting, a _____ is the value of money that has been used up to produce something, and hence is not available for use anymore. In economics, a _____ is an alternative that is given up as a result of a decision. In business, the _____ may be one of acquisition, in which case the amount of money expended to acquire it is counted as _____.
    a. Cost
    b. Fixed costs
    c. Variable cost
    d. Transaction cost

Chapter 7. Database and Customer Data Development

1. _____ is a method used for analyzing customer behavior and defining market segments. It is commonly used in database marketing and direct marketing and has received particular attention in retail.

   _____ stands for

   - Recency - When was the last order?
   - Frequency - How many orders have they placed with us?
   - Monetary Value - What is the value of their orders?

   To create an _____ analysis, one creates categories for each attribute. For instance, the Recency attribute might be broken into three categories: customers with purchases within the last 90 days; between 91 and 365 days; and longer than 365 days.

   a. Retail loss prevention
   b. Trade credit
   c. Merchant
   d. RFM

2. _____ refer to a collection of facts usually collected as the result of experience, observation or experiment or a set of premises. This may consist of numbers, words particularly as measurements or observations of a set of variables. _____ are often viewed as a lowest level of abstraction from which information and knowledge are derived.
   a. Data
   b. Sample size
   c. Pearson product-moment correlation coefficient
   d. Mean

3. A _____ is a structured collection of records or data that is stored in a computer system. The structure is achieved by organizing the data according to a _____ model. The model in most common use today is the relational model.
   a. 180SearchAssistant
   b. Power III
   c. 6-3-5 Brainwriting
   d. Database

4. _____ is the process of extracting hidden patterns from data. As more data is gathered, with the amount of data doubling every three years, _____ is becoming an increasingly important tool to transform this data into information. It is commonly used in a wide range of profiling practices, such as marketing, surveillance, fraud detection and scientific discovery.

a. Power III
b. Structure mining
c. 180SearchAssistant
d. Data mining

5. _____ constitute a class of computer-based information systems including knowledge-based systems that support decision-making activities.

_____ are a specific class of computerized information system that supports business and organizational decision-making activities. A properly-designed _____ is an interactive software-based system intended to help decision makers compile useful information from raw data, documents, personal knowledge, and/or business models to identify and solve problems and make decisions.

a. 180SearchAssistant
b. 6-3-5 Brainwriting
c. Power III
d. Decision support systems

6. '_____' is a class of statistical techniques that can be applied to data that exhibit 'natural' groupings. _____ sorts through the raw data and groups them into clusters. A cluster is a group of relatively homogeneous cases or observations.
a. Cluster analysis
b. 180SearchAssistant
c. Structure mining
d. Power III

7. An _____ is the manufacturing of a good or service within a category. Although _____ is a broad term for any kind of economic production, in economics and urban planning _____ is a synonym for the secondary sector, which is a type of economic activity involved in the manufacturing of raw materials into goods and products.

There are four key industrial economic sectors: the primary sector, largely raw material extraction industries such as mining and farming; the secondary sector, involving refining, construction, and manufacturing; the tertiary sector, which deals with services (such as law and medicine) and distribution of manufactured goods; and the quaternary sector, a relatively new type of knowledge _____ focusing on technological research, design and development such as computer programming, and biochemistry.

Chapter 7. Database and Customer Data Development

   a. AMAX
   b. ACNielsen
   c. ADTECH
   d. Industry

8. _____ is an advertisement in which a particular product specifically mentions a competitor by name for the express purpose of showing why the competitor is inferior to the product naming it.

This should not be confused with parody advertisements, where a fictional product is being advertised for the purpose of poking fun at the particular advertisement, nor should it be confused with the use of a coined brand name for the purpose of comparing the product without actually naming an actual competitor. ('Wikipedia tastes better and is less filling than the Encyclopedia Galactica.')

In the 1980s, during what has been referred to as the cola wars, soft-drink manufacturer Pepsi ran a series of advertisements where people, caught on hidden camera, in a blind taste test, chose Pepsi over rival Coca-Cola.

   a. Heavy-up
   b. GL-70
   c. Cost per conversion
   d. Comparative advertising

9. A _____ is a type of wholesale merchant business that buys goods and bulk products from importers, other wholesalers and then sells to retailers. _____s can deal in any commodity destined for the retail market. Typical categories are food, lumber, hardware, fuel, and textiles.
   a. Refusal to deal
   b. Tacit collusion
   c. Jobbing house
   d. Chief privacy officer

10. A _____ is a business that is independently owned and operated, with a small number of employees and relatively low volume of sales. The legal definition of 'small' often varies by country and industry, but is generally under 100 employees in the United States and under 50 employees in the European Union. In comparison, the definition of mid-sized business by the number of employees is generally under 500 in the U.S. and 250 for the European Union.
   a. Product support
   b. Customer centricity
   c. Time to market
   d. Small business

Chapter 8. Sales Strategy and CRM

1. _____ is a method used for analyzing customer behavior and defining market segments. It is commonly used in database marketing and direct marketing and has received particular attention in retail.

   _____ stands for

   - Recency - When was the last order?
   - Frequency - How many orders have they placed with us?
   - Monetary Value - What is the value of their orders?

   To create an _____ analysis, one creates categories for each attribute. For instance, the Recency attribute might be broken into three categories: customers with purchases within the last 90 days; between 91 and 365 days; and longer than 365 days.

   a. Merchant
   b. Trade credit
   c. Retail loss prevention
   d. RFM

2. A _____ is a plan of action designed to achieve a particular goal.

   _____ is different from tactics. In military terms, tactics is concerned with the conduct of an engagement while _____ is concerned with how different engagements are linked.

   a. Strategy
   b. 6-3-5 Brainwriting
   c. Power III
   d. 180SearchAssistant

3. _____ is a broad label that refers to any individuals or households that use goods and services generated within the economy. The concept of a _____ is used in different contexts, so that the usage and significance of the term may vary.

   A _____ is a person who uses any product or service.

   a. 180SearchAssistant
   b. Power III
   c. 6-3-5 Brainwriting
   d. Consumer

4. In the field of computer security, _____ is the criminally fraudulent process of attempting to acquire sensitive information such as usernames, passwords and credit card details by masquerading as a trustworthy entity in an electronic communication. Communications purporting to be from popular social web sites, auction sites, online payment processors or IT Administrators are commonly used to lure the unsuspecting public. _____ is typically carried out by e-mail or instant messaging, and it often directs users to enter details at a fake website whose look and feel are almost identical to the legitimate one.
   a. Telemarketing
   b. Joe job
   c. Phishing
   d. Directory Harvest Attack

5. _____ is a retailing concept in which the total range of products sold by a retailer is broken down into discrete groups of similar or related products; these groups are known as product categories. Examples of grocery categories may be: tinned fish, washing detergent, toothpastes, etc. Each category is then run like a 'mini business' (Business Unit) in its own right, with its own set of turnover and/or profitability targets and strategies. An important facet of _____ is the shift in relationship between retailer and supplier : instead of the traditional adversarial relationship, the relationship moves to one of collaboration, exchange of information and data and joint business building. The focus of all negotiations is centered around the effects of the turnover of the total category, not just the sales on the individual products therein.
   a. Brochure
   b. Societal marketing
   c. Market segment
   d. Category management

6. An _____ is the manufacturing of a good or service within a category. Although _____ is a broad term for any kind of economic production, in economics and urban planning _____ is a synonym for the secondary sector, which is a type of economic activity involved in the manufacturing of raw materials into goods and products.

There are four key industrial economic sectors: the primary sector, largely raw material extraction industries such as mining and farming; the secondary sector, involving refining, construction, and manufacturing; the tertiary sector, which deals with services (such as law and medicine) and distribution of manufactured goods; and the quaternary sector, a relatively new type of knowledge _____ focusing on technological research, design and development such as computer programming, and biochemistry.

   a. ADTECH
   b. ACNielsen
   c. AMAX
   d. Industry

7. A _____ is a systematic approach to selling a product or service. A growing body of published literature approaches the _____ from the point of view of an engineering discipline

Chapter 8. Sales Strategy and CRM

Reasons for having a well thought-out _____ include seller and buyer risk management, standardized customer interaction in sales, and scalable revenue generation.

a. Request for proposal
b. Sales management
c. Lead generation
d. Sales process

8. _____ is the provision of service to customers before, during and after a purchase.

According to Turban et al., '_____ is a series of activities designed to enhance the level of customer satisfaction - that is, the feeling that a product or service has met the customer expectation.'

Its importance varies by product, industry and customer.

a. Facing
b. Customer experience
c. COPC Inc.
d. Customer service

9. _____ is an advertisement in which a particular product specifically mentions a competitor by name for the express purpose of showing why the competitor is inferior to the product naming it.

This should not be confused with parody advertisements, where a fictional product is being advertised for the purpose of poking fun at the particular advertisement, nor should it be confused with the use of a coined brand name for the purpose of comparing the product without actually naming an actual competitor. ('Wikipedia tastes better and is less filling than the Encyclopedia Galactica.')

In the 1980s, during what has been referred to as the cola wars, soft-drink manufacturer Pepsi ran a series of advertisements where people, caught on hidden camera, in a blind taste test, chose Pepsi over rival Coca-Cola.

a. Heavy-up
b. GL-70
c. Cost per conversion
d. Comparative advertising

10. _____ is the practice of individuals including commercial businesses, governments and institutions, facilitating the sale of their products or services to other companies or organizations that in turn resell them, use them as components in products or services they offer _____ is also called business-to-_____ for short. (Note that while marketing to government entities shares some of the same dynamics of organizational marketing, B2G Marketing is meaningfully different.)
   a. Mass marketing
   b. Law of disruption
   c. Disruptive technology
   d. Business marketing

Chapter 9. CRM Technology and Sales

1. _____ refer to a collection of facts usually collected as the result of experience, observation or experiment or a set of premises. This may consist of numbers, words particularly as measurements or observations of a set of variables. _____ are often viewed as a lowest level of abstraction from which information and knowledge are derived.
   a. Data
   b. Mean
   c. Pearson product-moment correlation coefficient
   d. Sample size

2. _____ is a method used for analyzing customer behavior and defining market segments. It is commonly used in database marketing and direct marketing and has received particular attention in retail.

   _____ stands for

   - Recency - When was the last order?
   - Frequency - How many orders have they placed with us?
   - Monetary Value - What is the value of their orders?

   To create an _____ analysis, one creates categories for each attribute. For instance, the Recency attribute might be broken into three categories: customers with purchases within the last 90 days; between 91 and 365 days; and longer than 365 days.

   a. Retail loss prevention
   b. RFM
   c. Trade credit
   d. Merchant

3. _____ is the practice of individuals including commercial businesses, governments and institutions, facilitating the sale of their products or services to other companies or organizations that in turn resell them, use them as components in products or services they offer _____ is also called business-to-_____ for short. (Note that while marketing to government entities shares some of the same dynamics of organizational marketing, B2G Marketing is meaningfully different.)
   a. Disruptive technology
   b. Law of disruption
   c. Mass marketing
   d. Business marketing

4. In the field of computer security, _____ is the criminally fraudulent process of attempting to acquire sensitive information such as usernames, passwords and credit card details by masquerading as a trustworthy entity in an electronic communication. Communications purporting to be from popular social web sites, auction sites, online payment processors or IT Administrators are commonly used to lure the unsuspecting public. _____ is typically carried out by e-mail or instant messaging, and it often directs users to enter details at a fake website whose look and feel are almost identical to the legitimate one.
   a. Telemarketing
   b. Joe job
   c. Phishing
   d. Directory Harvest Attack

5. _____ is the provision of service to customers before, during and after a purchase.

According to Turban et al., '_____ is a series of activities designed to enhance the level of customer satisfaction - that is, the feeling that a product or service has met the customer expectation.'

Its importance varies by product, industry and customer.

   a. Facing
   b. Customer service
   c. Customer experience
   d. COPC Inc.

6. _____ is an advertisement in which a particular product specifically mentions a competitor by name for the express purpose of showing why the competitor is inferior to the product naming it.

This should not be confused with parody advertisements, where a fictional product is being advertised for the purpose of poking fun at the particular advertisement, nor should it be confused with the use of a coined brand name for the purpose of comparing the product without actually naming an actual competitor. ('Wikipedia tastes better and is less filling than the Encyclopedia Galactica.')

In the 1980s, during what has been referred to as the cola wars, soft-drink manufacturer Pepsi ran a series of advertisements where people, caught on hidden camera, in a blind taste test, chose Pepsi over rival Coca-Cola.

   a. GL-70
   b. Heavy-up
   c. Comparative advertising
   d. Cost per conversion

Chapter 9. CRM Technology and Sales

7. Sales force management systems are information systems used in marketing and management that help automate some sales and sales force management functions. They are frequently combined with a marketing information system, in which case they are often called Customer Relationship Management (CRM) systems.

_____ Systems , typically a part of a company's customer relationship management system, is a system that automatically records all the stages in a sales process.

   a. 180SearchAssistant
   b. 6-3-5 Brainwriting
   c. Sales force automation
   d. Power III

8. _____ is the study of the Earth and its lands, features, inhabitants, and phenomena. A literal translation would be 'to describe or write about the Earth'. The first person to use the word '_____' was Eratosthenes .

   a. Power III
   b. 6-3-5 Brainwriting
   c. 180SearchAssistant
   d. Geography

9. _____ is the process of estimation in unknown situations. Prediction is a similar, but more general term. Both can refer to estimation of time series, cross-sectional or longitudinal data.

   a. Power III
   b. Forecasting
   c. 6-3-5 Brainwriting
   d. 180SearchAssistant

Chapter 10. Marketing Strategy and CRM

1. _____ is defined by the American _____ Association as the activity, set of institutions, and processes for creating, communicating, delivering, and exchanging offerings that have value for customers, clients, partners, and society at large. The term developed from the original meaning which referred literally to going to market, as in shopping, or going to a market to sell goods or services.

   _____ practice tends to be seen as a creative industry, which includes advertising, distribution and selling.

   a. Product naming
   b. Marketing myopia
   c. Customer acquisition management
   d. Marketing

2. A _____ is a process that can allow an organization to concentrate its limited resources on the greatest opportunities to increase sales and achieve a sustainable competitive advantage. A _____ should be centered around the key concept that customer satisfaction is the main goal.

   A _____ is most effective when it is an integral component of corporate strategy, defining how the organization will successfully engage customers, prospects, and competitors in the market arena.

   a. Psychographic
   b. Marketing strategy
   c. Cyberdoc
   d. Societal marketing

3. A _____ is a plan of action designed to achieve a particular goal.

   _____ is different from tactics. In military terms, tactics is concerned with the conduct of an engagement while _____ is concerned with how different engagements are linked.

   a. 6-3-5 Brainwriting
   b. 180SearchAssistant
   c. Power III
   d. Strategy

4. The loyalty business model is a business model used in strategic management in which company resources are employed so as to increase the loyalty of customers and other stakeholders in the expectation that corporate objectives will be met or surpassed. A typical example of this type of model is: quality of product or service leads to customer satisfaction, which leads to _____, which leads to profitability.

   Fredrick Reichheld (1996) expanded the loyalty business model beyond customers and employees.

a. Power III
b. 6-3-5 Brainwriting
c. 180SearchAssistant
d. Customer loyalty

5. _____, a business term, is a measure of how products and services supplied by a company meet or surpass customer expectation. It is seen as a key performance indicator within business and is part of the four perspectives of a Balanced Scorecard.

In a competitive marketplace where businesses compete for customers, _____ is seen as a key differentiator and increasingly has become a key element of business strategy.

a. Supplier diversity
b. Customer satisfaction
c. Customer base
d. Psychological pricing

6. _____ is an advertisement in which a particular product specifically mentions a competitor by name for the express purpose of showing why the competitor is inferior to the product naming it.

This should not be confused with parody advertisements, where a fictional product is being advertised for the purpose of poking fun at the particular advertisement, nor should it be confused with the use of a coined brand name for the purpose of comparing the product without actually naming an actual competitor. ('Wikipedia tastes better and is less filling than the Encyclopedia Galactica.')

In the 1980s, during what has been referred to as the cola wars, soft-drink manufacturer Pepsi ran a series of advertisements where people, caught on hidden camera, in a blind taste test, chose Pepsi over rival Coca-Cola.

a. Cost per conversion
b. GL-70
c. Heavy-up
d. Comparative advertising

7. In environmental modeling and especially in hydrology, a _____ model means a model that is acceptably consistent with observed natural processes, i.e. that simulates well, for example, observed river discharge. It is a key concept of the so-called Generalized Likelihood Uncertainty Estimation (GLUE) methodology to quantify how uncertain environmental predictions are.

a. 6-3-5 Brainwriting
b. Behavioral
c. 180SearchAssistant
d. Power III

8. Competitiveness is a comparative concept of the ability and performance of a firm, sub-sector or country to sell and supply goods and/or services in a given market. Although widely used in economics and business management, the usefulness of the concept, particularly in the context of national competitiveness, is vigorously disputed by economists, such as Paul Krugman .

The term may also be applied to markets, where it is used to refer to the extent to which the market structure may be regarded as perfectly _____.

a. Geographical pricing
b. Customs union
c. Free trade zone
d. Competitive

9. Radio-frequency identification (_____) is the use of an object (typically referred to as an _____ tag) applied to or incorporated into a product, animal, or person for the purpose of identification and tracking using radio waves. Some tags can be read from several meters away and beyond the line of sight of the reader.

Most _____ tags contain at least two parts.

a. Power III
b. 180SearchAssistant
c. 6-3-5 Brainwriting
d. RFID

10. _____ is a method used for analyzing customer behavior and defining market segments. It is commonly used in database marketing and direct marketing and has received particular attention in retail.

_____ stands for

- Recency - When was the last order?
- Frequency - How many orders have they placed with us?
- Monetary Value - What is the value of their orders?

Chapter 10. Marketing Strategy and CRM 41

To create an _____ analysis, one creates categories for each attribute. For instance, the Recency attribute might be broken into three categories: customers with purchases within the last 90 days; between 91 and 365 days; and longer than 365 days.

a. RFM
b. Trade credit
c. Retail loss prevention
d. Merchant

11. _____ is defined by the Oxford English Dictionary as 'the action or practice of selling among or between established clients, markets, traders, etc.' or 'that of selling an additional product or service to an existing customer'. In practice businesses define _____ in many different ways. Elements that might influence the definition might include: the size of the business, the industry sector it operates within and the financial motivations of those required to define the term.
a. Freebie marketing
b. Yield management
c. Cross-selling
d. Service provider

12. A personal and cultural _____ is a relative ethic _____, an assumption upon which implementation can be extrapolated. A _____ system is a set of consistent _____s and measures that is soo not true. A principle _____ is a foundation upon which other _____s and measures of integrity are based.
a. Value
b. Perceptual maps
c. Supreme Court of the United States
d. Package-on-Package

13. In the field of marketing, a customer _____ consists of the sum total of benefits which a vendor promises that a customer will receive in return for the customer's associated payment (or other value-transfer.)

Put simply, the _____ is what the customer gets for his money.

Accordingly, a customer can evaluate a company's value-proposition on two broad dimensions with multiple subsets:

1. relative performance: what the customer gets from the vendor relative to a competitor's offering;
2. price: which consists of the payment the customer makes to acquire the product or service; plus the access cost

The vendor-company's marketing and sales efforts offer a customer _____; the vendor-company's delivery and customer-service processes then fulfill that value-proposition.

A value-proposition can assist in a firm's marketing strategy, and may guide a business to target a particular market segment.

a. DefCom Australia
b. Value proposition
c. Relationship management
d. Marketing performance measurement and management

14. _____ is the activity that the selling organization undertakes to reduce customer account defections. The success of this activity is when the customer account places an additional order before a 12-month period has expired. Note that ideally these orders will need to contribute similar financial amounts to the previous 12 months.
a. Customer base
b. Customer retention
c. First-mover advantage
d. Customer centricity

15. _____s are structured marketing efforts that reward, and therefore encourage, loyal buying behaviour -- behaviour which is potentially of benefit to the firm.

In marketing generally and in retailing more specifically, a loyalty card, rewards card, points card, advantage card, or club card is a plastic or paper card, visually similar to a credit card or debit card, that identifies the card holder as a member in a _____. Loyalty cards are a system of the loyalty business model.

a. 180SearchAssistant
b. Loyalty program
c. Power III
d. 6-3-5 Brainwriting

16. On an intranet or B2E Enterprise Web portals, personalization is often based on user attributes such as department, functional area, or role. The term _____ in this context refers to the ability of users to modify the page layout or specify what content should be displayed.

There are two categories of personalizations:

1. Rule-based
2. Content-based

Web personalization models include rules-based filtering, based on 'if this, then that' rules processing, and collaborative filtering, which serves relevant material to customers by combining their own personal preferences with the preferences of like-minded others. Collaborative filtering works well for books, music, video, etc.

a. Cashmere Agency
b. Customization
c. Self branding
d. Movin'

17. _____ or personalisation is tailoring a consumer product, electronic or written medium to a user based on personal details or characteristics they provide. More recently, it has especially been applied in the context of the World Wide Web.

Web pages are personalized based on the interests of an individual.

a. Flighting
b. Complex sale
c. Sexism,
d. Personalization

18. _____ is the process by which a new idea or new product is accepted by the market. The rate of _____ is the speed that the new idea spreads from one consumer to the next. Adoption is similar to _____ except that it deals with the psychological processes an individual goes through, rather than an aggregate market process.

a. Diffusion
b. Market development
c. Perceptual maps
d. Kano model

Chapter 11. CRM, Marketing Automation, and Communication

1. _____ is defined by the American _____ Association as the activity, set of institutions, and processes for creating, communicating, delivering, and exchanging offerings that have value for customers, clients, partners, and society at large. The term developed from the original meaning which referred literally to going to market, as in shopping, or going to a market to sell goods or services.

_____ practice tends to be seen as a creative industry, which includes advertising, distribution and selling.

a. Marketing myopia
b. Product naming
c. Customer acquisition management
d. Marketing

2. Radio-frequency identification (_____) is the use of an object (typically referred to as an _____ tag) applied to or incorporated into a product, animal, or person for the purpose of identification and tracking using radio waves. Some tags can be read from several meters away and beyond the line of sight of the reader.

Most _____ tags contain at least two parts.

a. RFID
b. 6-3-5 Brainwriting
c. Power III
d. 180SearchAssistant

3. _____ refer to a collection of facts usually collected as the result of experience, observation or experiment or a set of premises. This may consist of numbers, words particularly as measurements or observations of a set of variables. _____ are often viewed as a lowest level of abstraction from which information and knowledge are derived.

a. Sample size
b. Pearson product-moment correlation coefficient
c. Data
d. Mean

4. _____ is systematic determination of merit, worth, and significance of something or someone using criteria against a set of standards. _____ often is used to characterize and appraise subjects of interest in a wide range of human enterprises, including the arts, criminal justice, foundations and non-profit organizations, government, health care, and other human services.

Depending on the topic of interest, there are professional groups which look to the quality and rigor of the _____ process.

a. AMAX
b. ADTECH
c. ACNielsen
d. Evaluation

Chapter 12. CRM Program Measurement and Tools

1.

The net present value (NPV) of all of a company's customers in terms of customer loyalty and indirectly, the revenue that the company can obtain from them.

In deciding the value of a company, it is important to know of how much value its customer base is in terms of future revenues. The greater the _____ , the more future revenue in the lifetime of its clients; this means that a company with a higher _____ can get more money from its customers on average than another company that is identical in all other characteristics.

a. Marginal revenue
b. Total cost
c. Product proliferation
d. Customer equity

2. _____ is a method used for analyzing customer behavior and defining market segments. It is commonly used in database marketing and direct marketing and has received particular attention in retail.

_____ stands for

- Recency - When was the last order?
- Frequency - How many orders have they placed with us?
- Monetary Value - What is the value of their orders?

To create an _____ analysis, one creates categories for each attribute. For instance, the Recency attribute might be broken into three categories: customers with purchases within the last 90 days; between 91 and 365 days; and longer than 365 days.

a. Merchant
b. Trade credit
c. Retail loss prevention
d. RFM

3. _____ is defined by the Oxford English Dictionary as 'the action or practice of selling among or between established clients, markets, traders, etc.' or 'that of selling an additional product or service to an existing customer'. In practice businesses define _____ in many different ways. Elements that might influence the definition might include: the size of the business, the industry sector it operates within and the financial motivations of those required to define the term.

a. Service provider
b. Freebie marketing
c. Yield management
d. Cross-selling

4. _____, a business term, is a measure of how products and services supplied by a company meet or surpass customer expectation. It is seen as a key performance indicator within business and is part of the four perspectives of a Balanced Scorecard.

In a competitive marketplace where businesses compete for customers, _____ is seen as a key differentiator and increasingly has become a key element of business strategy.

a. Customer satisfaction
b. Customer base
c. Supplier diversity
d. Psychological pricing

5. _____ is an advertisement in which a particular product specifically mentions a competitor by name for the express purpose of showing why the competitor is inferior to the product naming it.

This should not be confused with parody advertisements, where a fictional product is being advertised for the purpose of poking fun at the particular advertisement, nor should it be confused with the use of a coined brand name for the purpose of comparing the product without actually naming an actual competitor. ('Wikipedia tastes better and is less filling than the Encyclopedia Galactica.')

In the 1980s, during what has been referred to as the cola wars, soft-drink manufacturer Pepsi ran a series of advertisements where people, caught on hidden camera, in a blind taste test, chose Pepsi over rival Coca-Cola.

a. Heavy-up
b. Cost per conversion
c. GL-70
d. Comparative advertising

6. In the field of computer security, _____ is the criminally fraudulent process of attempting to acquire sensitive information such as usernames, passwords and credit card details by masquerading as a trustworthy entity in an electronic communication. Communications purporting to be from popular social web sites, auction sites, online payment processors or IT Administrators are commonly used to lure the unsuspecting public. _____ is typically carried out by e-mail or instant messaging, and it often directs users to enter details at a fake website whose look and feel are almost identical to the legitimate one.

a. Directory Harvest Attack
b. Joe job
c. Telemarketing
d. Phishing

7. In economics, business, retail, and accounting, a _____ is the value of money that has been used up to produce something, and hence is not available for use anymore. In economics, a _____ is an alternative that is given up as a result of a decision. In business, the _____ may be one of acquisition, in which case the amount of money expended to acquire it is counted as _____.

   a. Transaction cost
   b. Fixed costs
   c. Variable cost
   d. Cost

8. In mathematics, an _____, or central tendency of a data set refers to a measure of the 'middle' or 'expected' value of the data set. There are many different descriptive statistics that can be chosen as a measurement of the central tendency of the data items.

   An _____ is a single value that is meant to typify a list of values.

   a. AMAX
   b. ACNielsen
   c. ADTECH
   d. Average

9. A _____ is a collection of symbols, experiences and associations connected with a product, a service, a person or any other artifact or entity.

   _____s have become increasingly important components of culture and the economy, now being described as 'cultural accessories and personal philosophies'.

   Some people distinguish the psychological aspect of a _____ from the experiential aspect.

   a. Brandable software
   b. Brand
   c. Store brand
   d. Brand equity

Chapter 12. CRM Program Measurement and Tools

10. _____ refers to the marketing effects or outcomes that accrue to a product with its brand name compared with those that would accrue if the same product did not have the brand name . And, at the root of these marketing effects is consumers' knowledge. In other words, consumers' knowledge about a brand makes manufacturers/advertisers respond differently or adopt appropriately adapt measures for the marketing of the brand .
   a. Brand image
   b. Brand aversion
   c. Product extension
   d. Brand equity

11. A personal and cultural _____ is a relative ethic _____, an assumption upon which implementation can be extrapolated. A _____ system is a set of consistent _____s and measures that is soo not true. A principle _____ is a foundation upon which other _____s and measures of integrity are based.
   a. Package-on-Package
   b. Supreme Court of the United States
   c. Perceptual maps
   d. Value

12. _____ is defined by the American _____ Association as the activity, set of institutions, and processes for creating, communicating, delivering, and exchanging offerings that have value for customers, clients, partners, and society at large. The term developed from the original meaning which referred literally to going to market, as in shopping, or going to a market to sell goods or services.

_____ practice tends to be seen as a creative industry, which includes advertising, distribution and selling.

   a. Customer acquisition management
   b. Marketing
   c. Product naming
   d. Marketing myopia

13. Consumer market research is a form of applied sociology that concentrates on understanding the behaviours, whims and preferences, of consumers in a market-based economy, and aims to understand the effects and comparative success of marketing campaigns. The field of consumer _____ as a statistical science was pioneered by Arthur Nielsen with the founding of the ACNielsen Company in 1923 .

Thus _____ is the systematic and objective identification, collection, analysis, and dissemination of information for the purpose of assisting management in decision making related to the identification and solution of problems and opportunities in marketing.

a. Logit analysis
b. Focus group
c. Marketing research process
d. Marketing research

14. _____ is the study of when, why, how, where and what people do or do not buy products. It blends elements from psychology, sociology, social psychology, anthropology and economics. It attempts to understand the buyer decision making process, both individually and in groups. It studies characteristics of individual consumers such as demographics and behavioural variables in an attempt to understand people's wants. It also tries to assess influences on the consumer from groups such as family, friends, reference groups, and society in general.
   a. Multidimensional scaling
   b. Communal marketing
   c. Consumer behavior
   d. Consumer confidence

15. _____ refer to a collection of facts usually collected as the result of experience, observation or experiment or a set of premises. This may consist of numbers, words particularly as measurements or observations of a set of variables. _____ are often viewed as a lowest level of abstraction from which information and knowledge are derived.
   a. Data
   b. Sample size
   c. Mean
   d. Pearson product-moment correlation coefficient

16. In statistics, an _____ draws inferences about the effect of a treatment on subjects, where the assignment of subjects into a treated group versus a control group is outside the control of the investigator. This is in contrast with controlled experiments, such as randomized controlled trials, where each subject is randomly assigned to a treated group or a control group before the start of the treatment.

Chapter 12. CRM Program Measurement and Tools

The assignment of treatments may be beyond the control of the investigator for a variety of reasons:

- A randomized experiment would violate ethical standards. Suppose one wanted to investigate the abortion-breast cancer hypothesis, which postulates a causal link between induced abortion and the incidence of breast cancer. In a hypothetical controlled experiment, one would start with a large subject pool of pregnant women and divide them randomly into a treatment group (receiving induced abortions) and a control group (bearing children), and then conduct regular cancer screenings for women from both groups. Needless to say, such an experiment would run counter to common ethical principles. (It would also suffer from various confounds and sources of bias, e.g., it would be impossible to conduct it as a blind experiment.) The published studies investigating the abortion-breast cancer hypothesis generally start with a group of women who already have received abortions. Membership in this 'treated' group is not controlled by the investigator: the group is formed after the 'treatment' has been assigned.

- The investigator may simply lack the requisite influence. Suppose a scientist wants to study the public health effects of a community-wide ban on smoking in public indoor areas.

a. ADTECH
b. AMAX
c. ACNielsen
d. Observational study

17. _____ is the sum of all experiences a customer has with a supplier of goods or services, over the duration of their relationship with that supplier. It can also be used to mean an individual experience over one transaction; the distinction is usually clear in context.

Analysts and commentators who write about _____ and CRM have increasingly recognized the importance of managing the customer's experience.

a. Customer experience
b. Customer service
c. Customer Integrated System
d. COPC Inc.

18. In statistics, an _____ is a term in a statistical model added when the effect of two or more variables is not simply additive. Such a term reflects that the effect of one variable depends on the values of one or more other variables.

Thus, for a response Y and two variables x_1 and x_2 an additive model would be:

$$Y = ax_1 + bx_2 + \text{error}$$

In contrast to this,

$$Y = ax_1 + bx_2 + c(x_1 \times x_2) + \text{error},$$

is an example of a model with an _____ between variables x_1 and x_2 ('error' refers to the random variable whose value by which y differs from the expected value of y.)

a. Interaction
b. AMAX
c. ACNielsen
d. ADTECH

19. A _____ is a list of the general tasks and responsibilities of a position. Typically, it also includes to whom the position reports, specifications such as the qualifications needed by the person in the job, salary range for the position, etc. A _____ is usually developed by conducting a job analysis, which includes examining the tasks and sequences of tasks necessary to perform the job.

a. Power III
b. 180SearchAssistant
c. 6-3-5 Brainwriting
d. Job description

Chapter 13. Privacy and Ethics Considerations

1. _____ is a branch of philosophy which seeks to address questions about morality, such as how a moral outcome can be achieved in a specific situation (applied _____), how moral values should be determined (normative _____), what moral values people actually abide by (descriptive _____), what the fundamental semantic, ontological, and epistemic nature of _____ or morality is (meta-_____), and how moral capacity or moral agency develops and what its nature is (moral psychology.)

Socrates was one of the first Greek philosophers to encourage both scholars and the common citizen to turn their attention from the outside world to the condition of man. In this view, Knowledge having a bearing on human life was placed highest, all other knowledge being secondary.

   a. AMAX
   b. ADTECH
   c. Ethics
   d. ACNielsen

2. _____ is the ability of an individual or group to seclude themselves or information about themselves and thereby reveal themselves selectively. The boundaries and content of what is considered private differ among cultures and individuals, but share basic common themes. _____ is sometimes related to anonymity, the wish to remain unnoticed or unidentified in the public realm.
   a. Privacy
   b. 6-3-5 Brainwriting
   c. 180SearchAssistant
   d. Power III

3. In the field of computer security, _____ is the criminally fraudulent process of attempting to acquire sensitive information such as usernames, passwords and credit card details by masquerading as a trustworthy entity in an electronic communication. Communications purporting to be from popular social web sites, auction sites, online payment processors or IT Administrators are commonly used to lure the unsuspecting public. _____ is typically carried out by e-mail or instant messaging, and it often directs users to enter details at a fake website whose look and feel are almost identical to the legitimate one.
   a. Telemarketing
   b. Joe job
   c. Phishing
   d. Directory Harvest Attack

4. _____ is the practice of individuals including commercial businesses, governments and institutions, facilitating the sale of their products or services to other companies or organizations that in turn resell them, use them as components in products or services they offer _____ is also called business-to-_____ for short. (Note that while marketing to government entities shares some of the same dynamics of organizational marketing, B2G Marketing is meaningfully different.)

Chapter 13. Privacy and Ethics Considerations

a. Disruptive technology
b. Mass marketing
c. Law of disruption
d. Business marketing

5. _____ is an advertisement in which a particular product specifically mentions a competitor by name for the express purpose of showing why the competitor is inferior to the product naming it.

This should not be confused with parody advertisements, where a fictional product is being advertised for the purpose of poking fun at the particular advertisement, nor should it be confused with the use of a coined brand name for the purpose of comparing the product without actually naming an actual competitor. ('Wikipedia tastes better and is less filling than the Encyclopedia Galactica.')

In the 1980s, during what has been referred to as the cola wars, soft-drink manufacturer Pepsi ran a series of advertisements where people, caught on hidden camera, in a blind taste test, chose Pepsi over rival Coca-Cola.

a. Comparative advertising
b. GL-70
c. Heavy-up
d. Cost per conversion

6. _____ is a broad label that refers to any individuals or households that use goods and services generated within the economy. The concept of a _____ is used in different contexts, so that the usage and significance of the term may vary.

A _____ is a person who uses any product or service.

a. Power III
b. 6-3-5 Brainwriting
c. 180SearchAssistant
d. Consumer

7. _____ is a form of communication that typically attempts to persuade potential customers to purchase or to consume more of a particular brand of product or service. 'While now central to the contemporary global economy and the reproduction of global production networks, it is only quite recently that _____ has been more than a marginal influence on patterns of sales and production. The formation of modern _____ was intimately bound up with the emergence of new forms of monopoly capitalism around the end of the 19th and beginning of the 20th century as one element in corporate strategies to create, organize and where possible control markets, especially for mass produced consumer goods.

Chapter 13. Privacy and Ethics Considerations

a. ADTECH
b. Advertising
c. AMAX
d. ACNielsen

8. The term _____ refers to several methods by which individuals can avoid receiving unsolicited product or service information. This ability is usually associated with direct marketing campaigns such as telemarketing, e-mail marketing, or direct mail.

The U.S. Federal Government created the National Do Not Call Registry to reduce the telemarketing calls consumers receive at home.

a. AMAX
b. Opt-out
c. ACNielsen
d. ADTECH

9. _____ refer to a collection of facts usually collected as the result of experience, observation or experiment or a set of premises. This may consist of numbers, words particularly as measurements or observations of a set of variables. _____ are often viewed as a lowest level of abstraction from which information and knowledge are derived.

a. Sample size
b. Mean
c. Pearson product-moment correlation coefficient
d. Data

10. Human beings are also considered to be _____ because they have the ability to change raw materials into valuable _____. The term Human _____ can also be defined as the skills, energies, talents, abilities and knowledge that are used for the production of goods or the rendering of services. While taking into account human beings as _____, the following things have to be kept in mind:

- The size of the population
- The capabilities of the individuals in that population

Many _____ cannot be consumed in their original form. They have to be processed in order to change them into more usable commodities.

a. Resources
b. 180SearchAssistant
c. Power III
d. 6-3-5 Brainwriting

Chapter 14. The Future of CRM

1. A _____ is a plan of action designed to achieve a particular goal.

   _____ is different from tactics. In military terms, tactics is concerned with the conduct of an engagement while _____ is concerned with how different engagements are linked.

   a. Power III
   b. 180SearchAssistant
   c. 6-3-5 Brainwriting
   d. Strategy

2. _____ is the process of estimation in unknown situations. Prediction is a similar, but more general term. Both can refer to estimation of time series, cross-sectional or longitudinal data.
   a. 6-3-5 Brainwriting
   b. Forecasting
   c. 180SearchAssistant
   d. Power III

3. _____ is difficult to define. For example, in 1952, Alfred Kroeber and Clyde Kluckhohn compiled a list of 164 definitions of '_____' in _____: A Critical Review of Concepts and Definitions. However, the word '_____' is most commonly used in three basic senses:

   - excellence of taste in the fine arts and humanities
   - an integrated pattern of human knowledge, belief, and behavior that depends upon the capacity for symbolic thought and social learning
   - the set of shared attitudes, values, goals, and practices that characterizes an institution, organization or group.

   When the concept first emerged in eighteenth- and nineteenth-century Europe, it connoted a process of cultivation or improvement, as in agriculture or horticulture. In the nineteenth century, it came to refer first to the betterment or refinement of the individual, especially through education, and then to the fulfillment of national aspirations or ideals.

   a. Culture
   b. African Americans
   c. Albert Einstein
   d. AStore

4. _____ refer to a collection of facts usually collected as the result of experience, observation or experiment or a set of premises. This may consist of numbers, words particularly as measurements or observations of a set of variables. _____ are often viewed as a lowest level of abstraction from which information and knowledge are derived.

a. Sample size
b. Pearson product-moment correlation coefficient
c. Mean
d. Data

ANSWER KEY

Chapter 1
1. a 2. b 3. d 4. d 5. a 6. a 7. d 8. d 9. b 10. b
11. c 12. d 13. a 14. d 15. d 16. d 17. d 18. d 19. d 20. c
21. d 22. b 23. c

Chapter 2
1. c 2. d 3. a 4. d 5. c 6. c 7. d 8. c 9. c 10. c
11. b 12. b 13. d 14. d 15. b 16. a 17. d 18. d

Chapter 3
1. d 2. a 3. a 4. b 5. b 6. d 7. d 8. a 9. d 10. c
11. c

Chapter 4
1. d 2. c 3. d 4. d 5. d 6. d 7. d

Chapter 5
1. d 2. d 3. a 4. c 5. d 6. d 7. d 8. d 9. d

Chapter 6
1. d 2. d 3. d 4. d 5. d 6. b 7. c 8. d 9. d 10. d
11. d 12. d 13. b 14. a

Chapter 7
1. d 2. a 3. d 4. d 5. d 6. a 7. d 8. d 9. c 10. d

Chapter 8
1. d 2. a 3. d 4. c 5. d 6. d 7. d 8. d 9. d 10. d

Chapter 9
1. a 2. b 3. d 4. c 5. b 6. c 7. c 8. d 9. b

Chapter 10
1. d 2. b 3. d 4. d 5. b 6. d 7. b 8. d 9. d 10. a
11. c 12. a 13. b 14. b 15. b 16. b 17. d 18. a

Chapter 11
1. d 2. a 3. c 4. d

Chapter 12
1. d 2. d 3. d 4. a 5. d 6. d 7. d 8. d 9. b 10. d
11. d 12. b 13. d 14. c 15. a 16. d 17. a 18. a 19. d

Chapter 13
1. c 2. a 3. c 4. d 5. a 6. d 7. b 8. b 9. d 10. a

Chapter 14
    1. d   2. b   3. a   4. d

www.ingramcontent.com/pod-product-compliance
Lightning Source LLC
Chambersburg PA
CBHW080743250426
43671CB00038B/2852